My Stories, My World

My World

A Grandma's Guided Journal

ISBN: 978-1-7373361-9-8

Storyopolis Press
Storyopolis Ventures LLC
66 West Flagler Street, Ste 900-3272 Miami, FL 33130
www.storyopolis.co

Printed in the United States of America

Contents

How to Use this Journal

This journal is intended to help you share your story. But we realize that your story is more than just a series of dates, events, parents, cousins, and great aunts and uncles. Your story is the world that you saw, heard about, and experienced.

Your story connects you to the many pieces of history that you've traveled through. Your words capture and preserve memories of personal and family milestones: births, weddings, graduations, childhood friendships, first pets, and first loves. We provide you with space, organizers, and images to help you record and describe how you felt about the people, events, products, movies, songs, books, and discoveries that shaped each stage of your life. Your view of history is unique and reveals a new side of you and your life to your readers—family, children, grandchildren, friends, and community members.

Your History Matters

For your children, grandchildren, and yet-to-be-born great-grandchildren, the history that you have experienced firsthand matters more than ever. You remember a pre-Internet, analogue world. You've lived through devastating wars and natural disasters, scientific breakthroughs, bizarre fashion trends, sports records and victories, and music that defined generations. Your firsthand descriptions provide vivid images and a very personal context that your children and grandchildren won't learn about in school or from history books. Whether you have traveled the world or lived on the same street your entire life, you offer unique memories that can shape your family's values, understanding, and views of the world. In twenty, thirty, or even forty years, your children and grandchildren may not remember the dates and historical details that they learned in school. But they will remember stories that Grandma told them about history. I certainly do, and you probably do too.

Before my teachers taught us about World War II and the Depression, I had heard the stories from my grandparents. Not a series of dates and policies but how it felt, how it tasted. I had heard about the summers of fun before hard times hit. The hardships, the losses, the enemies and dangers—some imagined and some very real. I saw their eyes spark when they remembered their heroes and idols as if they were my age again.

Decades later, my image of D-Day isn't just a paragraph in a textbook or a scene from a movie. The panic and uncertainty on Black Friday in 1929 takes on the tension that my grandfather remembered. And I still remember my grandmother's sly smile when she recalled Elvis on the *Ed Sullivan Show*. These stories add richness to our children's and grandchildren's sense of history. They also create a deeper, more complex picture of who grandparents actually are. Use our journal to let your children and grandchildren know you better through your stories.

Instructions for Grandparents

Our journals help grandparents organize their stories. They provide family trees, but they also provide a timeline that lets you walk your family through your life. We provide prompts and questions to help jog your memory and craft short, memorable stories and anecdotes about your different periods, events, and people in your life.

Sections of our journal help you capture your experiences during the decades that you lived. We provide images of important historical events, people, trends, music, movies, products, and inventions that defined eras. Within each time period, you choose the specific events, people, and topics that had the most influence on you. You explain the significance, feelings, and impact of these forces that shaped your life during each decade. This is how you interacted with the world during each period of your life. These are your stories and the history of your world.

Your stories help your children and grandchildren understand your views, beliefs, and values. But the stories that you're writing just begin here. They form the prompts for your family members to ask their own questions like, "Then what happened?" "Why did they do that?" "Why did you react that way?" and "Could that happen again?"

Some grandparents begin their story at the front of the journal. Others start by sharing details from the middle or latter part of their lives. You can come back to sections later or skip certain parts completely. Quite a few grandparents have told their stories and had their children and grandchildren write them in their journals for them. Story-sharing can become a wonderful, educational family activity. Take this opportunity to make memories for and with your family.

Instructions for Children and Grandchildren

Have you imagined your parents or grandparents when they were your age? Their world was very different from yours. But your grandparents' fears, hopes, dreams, and friendships weren't. Your grandparents lived through the history that you hear about in school. They saw World War II, the Apollo Moonwalk, the Civil Rights Movement, music, movies, and fun before the Internet and before the smartphone. Your grandparents' stories are personal. You won't learn about them from your teachers. You won't see them in movies or videos.

Some grandparents have the time and talent for telling great stories. Other grandparents may not. Our journal helps any grandparent tell more powerful, vivid, and memorable stories. By encouraging your grandparents to complete this journal, you can help them release their stories and bring them to life. You can read and ask questions. You can share what you learn about with your friends and schoolmates.

Instructions for School, Community, and Religious Groups

Schools, communities, and religious groups can uncover valuable experiences buried in the stories and memories of their eldest members. Some older members of your community are just waiting to be asked to share important lessons that they've gathered over decades. Others would love to share, but they don't know how.

Our journal creates the foundation for amazing community storytelling and sharing projects. Older members can write down their own views and experiences about historical events that are uniquely relevant to your community. Or younger members of the community can use our journal's prompts and questions to conduct guided interviews with seniors. The journal's questions can focus on local events that shaped your school or church, or bigger, global events like the Holocaust, the Civil Rights Movement, 9/11, or domestic conflict in the UK.

These journalized stories not only engage and include older members, but they also generate powerful and instructive dialogues and discussion topics across generations.

Join Our Living History Community and Share Your History

Learn how to share pieces of your history with fellow readers. Visit our website www.mystoriesmyworld.com and follow My Stories, My World on Facebook and Instagram. Find tips and resources to refresh your memory of facts, dates, and even the price of a home, a car, or a movie ticket when you were young. Discover how you can post and share anecdotes and stories from your journal.

My Place in History

I'm going to share many important stories from my life. But I also want you to know about family members that came before me. My parents, grandparents, uncles, aunts, and siblings shared experiences, memories, and values that shaped how I've lived my life and viewed history.

- Today, I'm _____ years old.

- I was born on _____ ____, _____ in _____, _____, _____
  (month) (day) (year)   (city)   (state/province) (country)

- My full name at birth was _____

- My name is special because _____

  _____

  (*Were you named after anyone, or does your name have a specific significance?*)

- When I was young, my nickname was _____

  because _____

  _____

  (*How did you get your nickname?*)

- Our family ancestors came from _____

  (*Which country, city, or area?*)

- We followed religious traditions that included _____

  _____

  _____

  _____

🖋 Family traditions, foods, stories, or music that connected me to my heritage included

_____

_____

_____

🖋 Our family has a history of medical conditions or genetic disorders that include

_____

_____

_____

_____

_____

_____

Grandma

_____

_____

_____

_____

_____

_____

_____

_____

_____

_____

_____

You

_____   _____

- My parents' names were _____ and _____

- My mother was born in _____ (*year/place*)

- Three words that I would use to describe my mother are

  _____, _____, _____

  because _____

  _____

  _____

- My mother worked as _____

- In her free time, my mother liked to _____

- A favorite story that my mother told me about her youth is:

  _____

  _____

  _____

- My father was born in _____ (*year/place*)

- Three words that I would use to describe my father are

  _____, _____, _____

  because _____

  _____

  _____

- My father worked as _____

- In his free time, my father liked to _____

- A favorite story that my father told me about his youth is:

  _____

  _____

  _____

🖋 I had brothers and sisters whose names were _____

🖋 I was the _____ (*oldest/youngest/second oldest/third oldest/etc.*)

🖋 A favorite memory of my sibling(s) is

_____

_____

_____

_____

_____

_____

_____

🖋 My father's parents, my paternal grandparents, names were

_____ and _____

🖋 My father's father was born in _____ (*year/place*)

🖋 My father's mother was born in _____

🖋 My paternal grandfather worked as _____

🖋 My paternal grandmother worked as _____

🖋 My favorite memory of my paternal grandmother is

_____

_____

_____

_____

_____

_____

🪶 My favorite memory of my paternal grandfather is

_____

_____

_____

_____

_____

_____

🪶 My mother's parents, my material grandparents, names were

_____ and _____

🪶 My mother's father was born in _____ (*year/place*)

🪶 My mother's mother was born in _____

🪶 My maternal grandfather worked as _____

🪶 My maternal grandmother worked as _____

🪶 My favorite memory of my maternal grandmother is

_____

_____

_____

_____

_____

_____

🖋 My favorite memory of my maternal grandfather is

_____

_____

_____

_____

_____

_____

🖋 I also was very close to my _____ named _____
   (*another relative, e.g. aunt, uncle, cousin, step-parent, etc.*)

🖋 My favorite memory of him or her is

_____

_____

_____

_____

_____

_____

🖋 A favorite story that my maternal/paternal grandfather told me about his youth is: (*circle one*)

_____

_____

_____

_____

_____

_____

A favorite story that my maternal/paternal grandmother told me about her youth is: *(circle one)*

_____

_____

_____

_____

_____

_____

My Journeys

On this map, I've highlighted important places that I've visited and lived in my journey through life. I've tried to identify places that my family and ancestors came from.

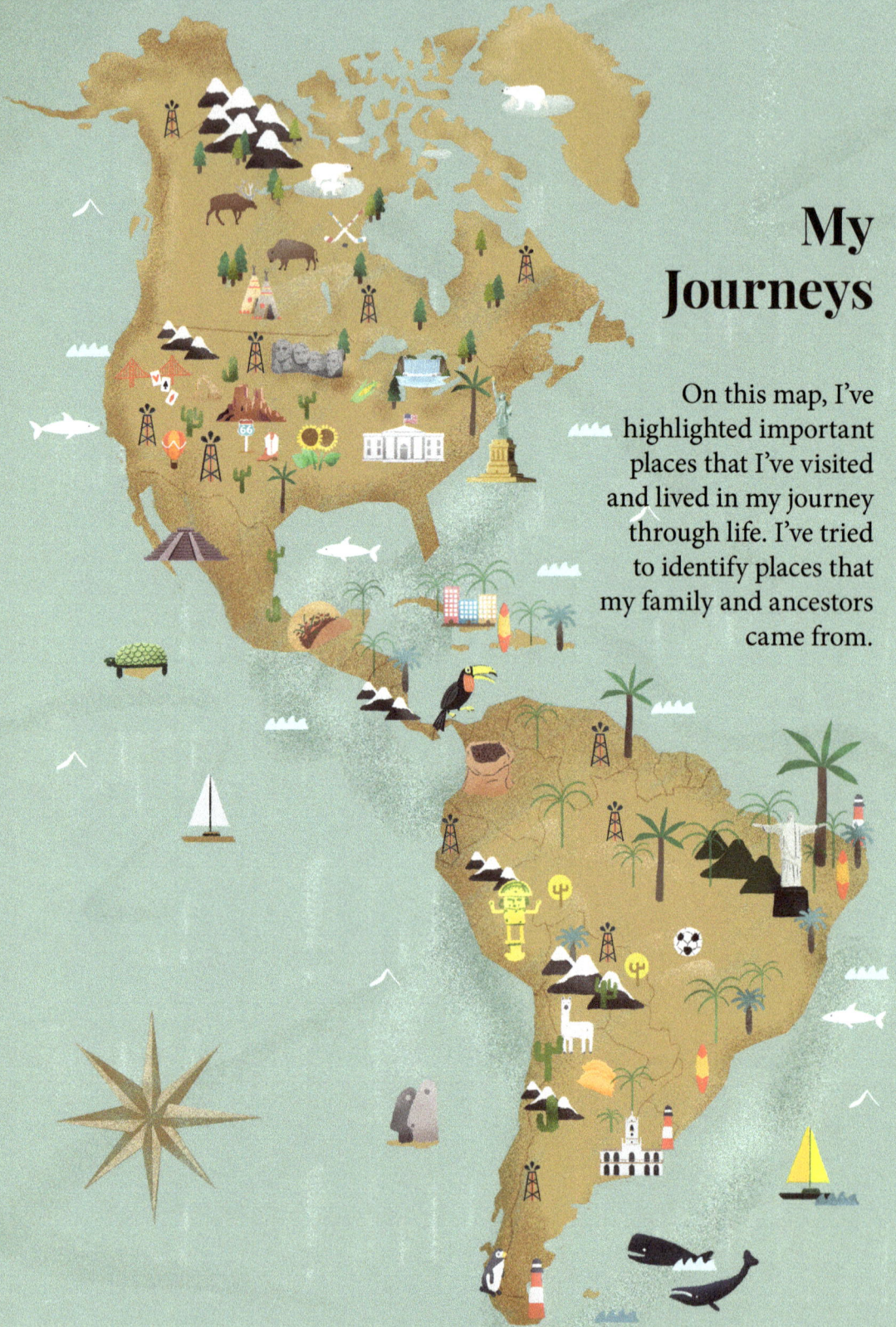

✕ where my ancestors came from   ○ memorable visits

△ where I was born   ✈ places that I still hope to visit

☐ places that I've lived

My Early Years

Instructions for writing this section. *Start by answering the questions about your life in your early childhood from the time of your birth until you were about twelve years old. Remember to include the years that this period of your life covered.*

After you have recorded the details and memories from your personal life, choose three memory prompts from the Moments in History section and copy each prompt onto one of the Memorable Moment lines in this section. Then, answer the prompt in the section below this Memorable Moment. The Moments in History that we have selected are only suggestions. You may add another important or historical event from this period of your life.

The goal of this section is to understand this period of history through your eyes. Some prompts list multiple people or things. You can choose one from these lists or add one of your own.

🖋 I was a young child during the years _____ to _____

🖋 When I was a young child, my favorite interests, hobbies, or sports were

_____

_____

🖋 When I was a young child, I had a pet _____ named _____.

🖋 A special memory about my pet is _____

_____

_____

_____

🖋 When I was a child, my best friend was _____.

A special memory about my friend is_____

_____

_____

_____

🖋 I went to _____ for primary school.

🖋 I went to _____ for middle school.

🖋 My favorite teacher was _____.

A special memory of this teacher is _____

_____

_____

_____

🖋 My favorite subjects in school were _____

🖋 A favorite memory from my early school years is

_____

_____

_____

_____

_____

_____

🖋 My schoolmates would describe me as

_____

_____

_____

_____

_____

_____

🖋 When I was young, I wanted to be a _____

when I grew up because _____

🖋 My favorite early family memory is _____

_____

_____

_____

_____

_____

_____

🖋 My favorite holiday memory from my childhood is _____

_____

_____

_____

_____

_____

_____

A favorite food from my early years was _____

One of the most important lessons that I learned during my early years was

_____

_____

_____

_____

_____

_____

The World in My Early Years

Life was much cheaper in my early years…

🖋 A house in my neighborhood cost _____

🖋 A car cost _____

🖋 Lunch at a restaurant that I might have visited cost _____

🖋 A movie ticket cost _____

Important historical events that influenced my early years included:

🖋 _____

🖋 _____

🖋 _____

🖋 _____

🖋 _____

Memorable Moment #1 from My Early Years

Copy one of the memory prompts on this line. Answer it below.

_____

_____

_____

_____

_____

_____

_____

_____

Memorable Moment #2 from My Early Years

Copy one of the memory prompts on this line. Answer it below.

_____

_____

_____

_____

_____

_____

_____

_____

Memorable Moment #3 from My Early Years

Copy one of the memory prompts on this line. Answer it below.

Moments in History: 1940s

The 1940s was a decade that transformed our world. Nations clashed. New, independent countries were born. Strong, determined leaders made tough decisions that shaped where and how I grew up. Women took on important new roles in the workforce. We listened and danced to swing. *Citizen Kane*, *Casablanca*, *Fantasia*, and *Bambi* made their mark on the big screen. TV with the *Ford Theater Hour*, *Milton Berle*, and *Tom and Jerry* were just starting to enter our homes. Let me share my memories of the events, people, products, sports, and art that came alive during this time.

1940s Memory Prompts

Choose three memory prompts below or use one of the important historical events that influenced this period of your life. Copy and answer the prompt as one of the three Memorable Moments that follow your personal memories for this period. If you were not born during this period but have memories that were shared with you by family members, you can include those as well. The goal of this section is to understand this period of history through your eyes. Some prompts list multiple people or things. You can choose one from these lists or add one of your own.

- A memory that I have about World War II is…

- A memory that I have about the Battle of Britain…

- A memory that I have about the attack on Pearl Harbor is…

- A memory that I have about President Franklin Roosevelt is…

- A memory that I have about Winston Churchill is…

- A memory that I have about India's independence is…

- A memory that I have about the founding of the People's Republic of China is…

- A memory that I have about the creation of the state of Israel is…

- A memory about a sports event or sports figure from the 1940s such as Stan Musial, Warren Spahn, Yogi Berra, Ted Williams, Jackie Robinson, Joe Louis, Sugar Ray Robinson, Jesse Owens, Joe DiMaggio, Stanley Matthews, Adolpho Pedernera, Telmo Zarra, is…

- A memory about a natural disaster that occurred in the 1940s is…

- A memory about a science or technology breakthrough in the 1940s such as penicillin, synthetic rubber, DDT, the Big Bang Theory, the atomic bomb, the jet plane, the transistor, the scuba diver's aqualung, radar, the helicopter, is…

- A memory about a new product that appeared in the 1940s such as Slinky, Tupperware, Velcro, the microwave, the Jeep, the Frisbee, ballpoint pen, bikinis, the modern jukebox, the Polaroid camera, aerosol spray cans, M&Ms, is…

- A memory about a popular movie star in the 1940s such as Humphrey Bogart, Lauren Bacall, William Holden, Ingrid Bergman, Cary Grant, Elizabeth Taylor, James Stewart, Clark Gable, Vivien Leigh, Lucille Ball, Natalie Wood, Lana Turner, is…

- A memory about a popular musician or band in the 1940s such as Ella Fitzgerald, The Andrew Sisters, Billie Holiday, Louis Armstrong, Tommy Dorsey, Benny Goodman, The Glenn Miller Orchestra, Bing Crosby, Frank Sinatra, is…

- A memory of a big social movement in the 1940s such as growth of women in the workforce, desegregation of the Armed Forces in the US, Japanese internment in the US, creation of the National Health Service in the United Kingdom, is…

citizen kane
pontiac streamliner fedora
howdy doody miracle on 34th street packard
ed sullivan woody station wagon
miracle on 34th street
swing woody station wagon
the maltese falcon
pillbox hat the transistor
white christmas pontiac streamliner velcro ella fitzgerald
citizen kane erector sets ed sullivan
louis armstrong swing packard
the little prince penicillin fantasia pillbox hat fantasia
the maltese falcon white christmas tiddlywinks the transistor native son
penicillin tupperware velcro
ella fitzgerald white christmas
native son tupperware howdy doody tiddlywinks
the lone ranger the little prince the lone ranger
fedora casablanca
casablanca

Moments in History: 1950s

The 1950s brought the Cold War. Families moved to new suburbs. Fitting in was "in". Popular musicians sowed the seeds for Rock and Roll. People traveled farther and faster by car and by plane. Disneyland opened. So did McDonald's. Sputnik and newly invented satellites made outer space look like it wasn't so far away. We watched *Ozzie and Harriet*, *Leave it to Beaver*, and *The Twilight Zone* in our living rooms. Let me share my memories of the events, people, products, sports, and art that shaped this decade.

marilyn monroe bill russell nasser buddy holly mickey mantle
mcdonald's barbie dolls rocky marciano joseph mccarthy
space race rocky marciano elvis presley iron curtain marilyn monroe daytona 500
teflon joseph mccarthy macarthur
yalu river joseph mccarthy dwight eisenhower jonas salk hula hoop mr. potato head
disneyland mcdonald's space race jonas salk mcdonald's
rock and roll daytona 500 teflon sputnik
warsaw pact iron curtain disneyland nasser satellite
elvis presley rock and roll mr. potato head mr. potato head satellite
rock hudson hula hoop iron curtain barbie dolls bill russell macarthur doo-wop
rocky marciano marilyn monroe jonas salk dwight eisenhower yalu river sputnik warsaw pact macarthur mcdonald's nasser
dwight eisenhower warsaw pact doo-wop teflon space race
yalu river disneyland chuck berry rock hudson marilyn monroe bill russell
bill russell daytona 500 elvis presley nasser satellite mickey mantle space race mickey mantle buddy holly
chuck berry satellite doo-wop chuck berry
rock hudson sputnik
doo-wop satellite
mcdonald's

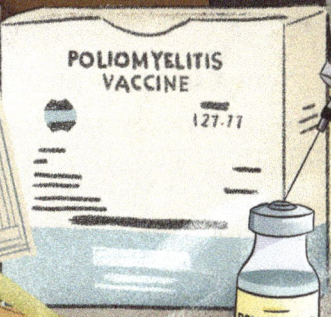

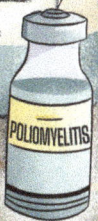

1950s Memory Prompts

Choose three memory prompts below or use one of the important historical events that influenced a period of your life. Copy and answer the prompt as one of the three Memorable Moments that follow your personal memories for this period. If you were not born during this period but have memories that were shared with you by family members, you can include those as well. The goal of this section is to understand this period of history through your eyes. Some prompts list multiple people or things. You can choose one from these lists or add one of your own.

- A memory about the Cold War or the Red Scare from the 1950s is...

- A memory about the Korean War is...

- A memory about the Suez Crisis is...

- A memory about the launch of Sputnik by the USSR is...

- A memory about the coronation of Queen Elizabeth II is...

- A memory about the Festival of Britain is...

- A memory about Salk's polio vaccine is...

- A memory about a sports event or sports figure from the 1950s such as Willie Mays, Rocky Marciano, Mickey Mantle, Jim Brown, Hank Aaron, Chuck Cooper, Wilt Chamberlain, Bill Russell, Alfredo Di Stéfano, Fritz Walter, John Charles, the Daytona 500 Car Race run for first time, is...

- A memory about a natural disaster that occurred in the 1950s such as Hurricane Barbara, the 1955 UK heat wave, the Great Appalachian Storm, is...

- A memory about a science or technology breakthrough in the 1950s such as the laser, the hovercraft, the integrated circuit, the pacemaker, Teflon, the satellite, is...

- A memory about a new product that appeared in the 1950s such as frozen dinners, dishwashers, the opening of Disneyland, hula hoops, Mr. Potato Head, credit cards, Barbie Dolls, high-fis with radios, McDonalds, the Austin Mini, passenger jets, is...

🖊 A memory about a popular movie star in the 1950s such as Charlton Heston, Rock Hudson, Dean Martin, Marilyn Monroe, John Wayne, Marlon Brando, Grace Kelly, Audrey Hepburn, Elizabeth Taylor, Shirley Maclaine is…

🖊 A memory about a popular musician or band in the 1950s such as Elvis Presley, Fats Domino, Buddy Holly, Ray Charles, Chuck Berry, Bill Haley & His Comets, Little Richard, The Everly Brothers, The Drifters, Tommy Steele, Johnny Cash, Hank Williams, is…

🖊 A memory of a big social movement in the 1950s such as Social Security introduced in the US, the US Labor Movement, the beginning of the Civil Rights Movement, the growth of suburbs, is…

My Teen Years

Instructions for writing this section. *Start by answering the questions about your life in your teen years. This period would be from the time that you were about thirteen until you were about twenty years old. For many people, their teen years covered the period from high school through college or the earliest period in their working lives. Remember to include the years that this period of your life covered.*

After you have recorded the details and memories from your personal life, choose three memory prompts from the Moments in History section and copy each prompt onto one of the Memorable Moment lines in this section. Then, answer the prompt in the section below this Memorable Moment. The Moments in History that we have selected are only suggestions. You may add another important or historical event from this period of your life.

The goal of this section is to understand this period of history through your eyes. Some prompts list multiple people or things. You can choose one from these lists or add one of your own.

🖋 My teen years were during the years _____ to _____

🖋 In my teen years, my favorite interests, hobbies, or sports were

_____

_____

🖋 In my teen years, I had a pet _____ named _____.

A special memory about my pet is _____

_____

_____

_____

_____

✐ In my teen years, my best friend was _____.

A special memory about my friend is_____

_____

_____

_____

_____

✐ I went to _____ for secondary school or high school.

✐ My favorite teacher in high school was _____.

A special memory of this teacher is _____

_____

_____

_____

_____

✐ My favorite subjects in high school were _____

✐ I dreamt about becoming a _____ when I grew up.

✐ I went to _____ for college or university. I studied _____

✐ My high school classmates would describe me as _____

_____

_____

_____

_____

✐ During my teen years, I often worried about _____

✐ My favorite family vacation when I was young was _____

_____

_____

One crazy thing that I did during my teen years was _____

_____

_____

If I could relive my teen years, something I could do differently would be

_____

_____

_____

_____

A favorite book from my teen years was _____

A favorite song from my teen years was _____

A favorite movie from my teen years was _____

One of the most important lessons that I learned during my teen years was

_____

_____

_____

_____

The World in My Teen Years

Life was much cheaper in my teen years…

- A house in my neighborhood cost _____

- A car cost _____

- Lunch at a restaurant that I might have visited cost _____

- A movie ticket cost _____

Important historical events that influenced my teen years included:

- _____

- _____

- _____

- _____

- _____

Memorable Moment #1 from My Teen Years

Copy one of the memory prompts on this line. Answer it below.

_____

_____

_____

_____

_____

_____

_____

Memorable Moment #2 from My Teen Years

Copy one of the memory prompts on this line. Answer it below.

_____

_____

_____

_____

_____

_____

_____

Memorable Moment #3 from My Teen Years

Copy one of the memory prompts on this line. Answer it below.

Moments in History: 1960s

The Civil Rights Movement, the Troubles, the Cuban Missile Crisis, and a war in Vietnam made the 1960s a decade that broke old molds. Leaders like John F. Kennedy and Martin Luther King Jr. made us think and dared us to hope and change our world. Astronauts walked on the moon. New music sensations rolled across the UK and the US. American football fans got their first Super Bowl. And James Bond made his first appearance at the movies. Let me share this decade's events, people, products, sports, and art that left their mark on me.

1960s Memory Prompts

Choose three memory prompts below or use one of the important historical events that influenced a period of your life. Copy and answer the prompt as one of the three Memorable Moments that follow your personal memories for this period. If you were not born during this period but have memories that were shared with you by family members, you can include those as well. The goal of this section is to understand this period of history through your eyes. Some prompts list multiple people or things. You can choose one from these lists or add one of your own.

- A memory about the Civil Rights Movement from the 1960s is…

- A memory about the Bay of Pigs or Cuban Missile Crisis is…

- A memory from the start of the Vietnam War or Anti-Vietnam War protests is…

- A memory about the Apollo moonwalk is…

- A memory about the Troubles in Ireland is…

- A memory about John F. Kennedy is…

- A memory about Martin Luther King Jr. is….

- A memory about the Prague Spring is…

- A memory about Prime Minister Harold MacMillan is…

- A memory about a sports event or sports figure from the 1960s such as Muhammed Ali, Sandy Koufax, Johnny Unitas, Wilt Chamberlain, Robert Maris, the first Super Bowl, Joe Namath, Billie Jean King, Arnold Palmer, the 1966 World Cup, George Best, Bobby Moore, Pele, is…

- A memory about a natural disaster that occurred in the 1960s such as the Anchorage earthquake, Hurricane Camille, the Chile earthquake and tsunami, is…

- A memory about a science or technology breakthrough in the 1960s such as the first human kidney transplant, the first human heart transplant, SEALAB expeditions, *Silent Spring's* warning about environmental hazards, BASIC computer language, is…

- A memory about a new product that appeared in the 1960s such as US zip codes, Sharpie pens, lava lamps, audio cassettes, Etch A Sketch, Easy Bake Ovens, child car seats, touch tone phones, music synthesizers, handheld calculators, soft contact lenses, vehicle safety belts, is…

- A memory about a popular movie star in the 1960s such as Paul Newman, Jack Lemmon, Steve McQueen, Sidney Poitier, Sean Connery, Julie Andrews, Richard Burton, Peter O'Toole, Natalie Wood, is…

- A memory about a popular musician or band in the 1960s such as The Beatles, The Rolling Stones, The Beach Boys, The Mamas and the Papas, Jimi Hendrix, Jefferson Airplane, The Doors, The Supremes, The Byrds, The Temptations, Bob Dylan, Aretha Franklin, is…

- A memory of a big social movement in the 1960s such as the launch of National Organization for Women, the Detroit and Watts riots, the Woodstock music festival, the Stonewall uprising, the creation of Medicaid/Medicare in the US, the founding of the American Indian Movement, is…

Moments in History: 1970s

The 1970s brought conflicts, conspiracies, protests, and new technology at home. Watergate shocked Americans. Bloody Sunday jolted the UK. The Yom Kippur War shook Israel. And the Oil Crisis hurt our wallets. Kids played Pong and Space Invaders while VCRs and personal computers made their way into our homes. Friends wore Sony Walkman headphones while they listened to new rock music or spun to the sounds of disco. Let me share the events, people, products, sports, and art that I remember best from the 1970s.

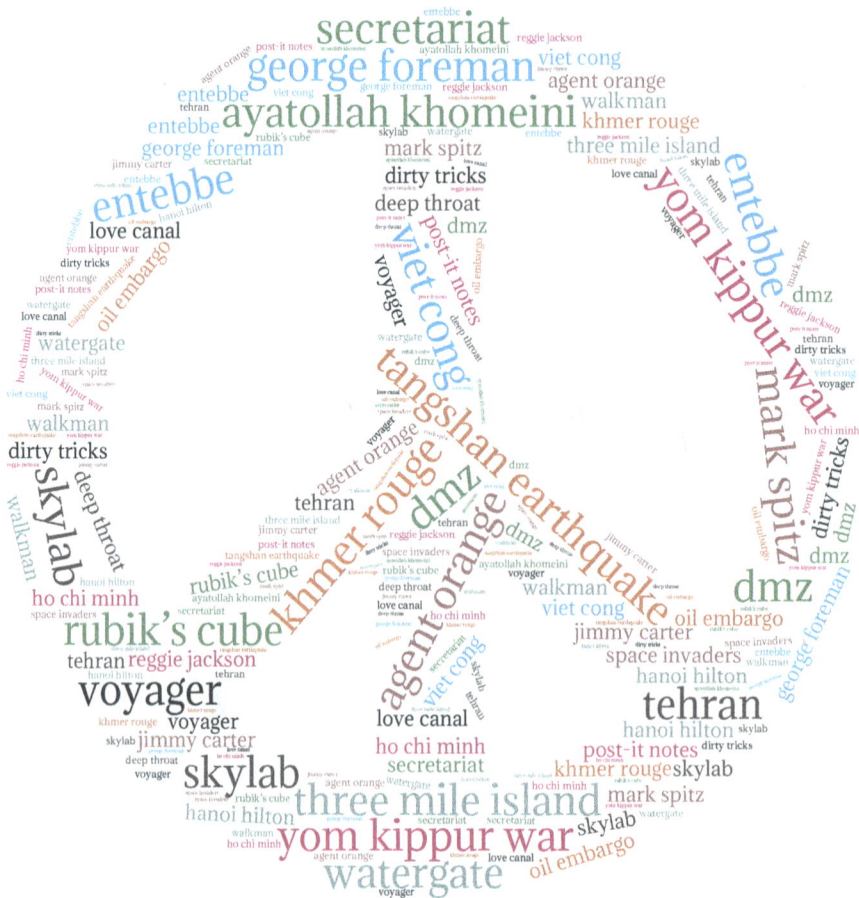

secretariat george foreman ayatollah khomeini entebbe love canal dirty tricks deep throat post-it notes viet cong voyager tangshan earthquake khmer rouge agent orange dmz three mile island walkman skylab rubik's cube reggie jackson ho chi minh tehran jimmy carter space invaders hanoi hilton yom kippur war mark spitz oil embargo watergate secretariat viet cong agent orange oil embargo yom kippur war mark spitz dmz watergate walkman dirty tricks skylab voyager three mile island post-it notes khmer rouge

1970s Memory Prompts

Choose three memory prompts below or use one of the important historical events that influenced a period of your life. Copy and answer the prompt as one of the three Memorable Moments that follow your personal memories for this period. The goal of this section is to understand this period of history through your eyes. Some prompts list multiple people or things. You can choose one from these lists or add one of your own.

- A memory about the end of the Vietnam War is…

- A memory about the Watergate scandal is…

- A memory about Bloody Sunday is…

- A memory about Queen Elizabeth's Silver Jubilee is…

- A memory about the 1970s oil crisis is…

- A memory about the Yom Kippur War is…

- A memory about the Iran hostage crisis is…

- A memory about the US Bicentennial celebration is…

- A memory of environmental disasters like Love Canal or Three Mile Island is…

- A memory about a sports event or sports figure from the 1970s such as the 1972 Olympics, Pete Rose, Reggie Jackson, Nolan Ryan, Rod Carew, Julius Erving, George Foreman, O.J. Simpson, Jack Nicklaus, Kareem Abdul-Jabbar, Richard Petty, Mark Spitz, Roger Staubach, Bobby Orr, Tom Seaver, Secretariat, Nadia Comaneci, is…

- A memory about a natural disaster that occurred in the 1970s such as Hurricane Agnes, the Great Peruvian earthquake, the Tangshan earthquake, is…

- A memory about a science or technology breakthrough in the 1970s such as the theory of black holes, the Voyager space mission, the MRI machine, the Skylab space station, is…

- A memory about a new product that appeared in the 1970s such as personal computers, floppy disks, digital wrist watches, Pong and Space Invaders video games, VCRs, cellphones, the Sony Walkman, the Boeing 747, Post-it Notes, Rubik's Cube, Jelly Bellys, Reese's Pieces, McDonald's Quarter Pounder is…

- A memory about a popular movie star in the 1970s such as Al Pacino, Dustin Hoffman, Robert De Niro, Robert Redford, Meryl Streep, Faye Dunaway, Diane Keaton, *Star Wars*, Harrison Ford, Clint Eastwood, Jane Fonda, Barbara Streisand, Woody Allen, Charles Bronson, is…

- A memory about a popular musician or band in the 1970s such as Elton John, Led Zeppelin, David Bowie, The Eagles, Pink Floyd, Fleetwood Mac, The Jackson 5, Diana Ross, The Bee Gees, The Who, Abba, Parliament-Funkadelic, Sly and the Family Stone, Marvin Gaye, Queen, Bob Marley, Dolly Parton, Joni Mitchell, is…

- A memory of a big social movement in the 1970s such as the launch of Earth Day, the Moral Majority, Women's Liberation and the Equal Rights Amendment, the Pentagon Papers, is…

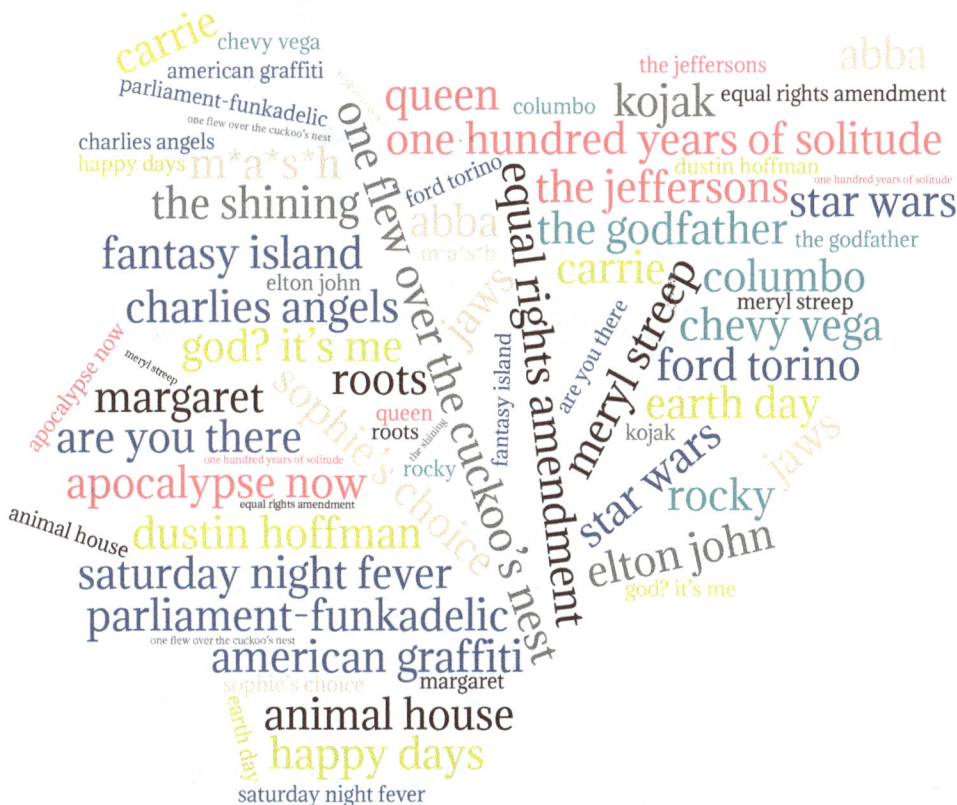

My Adult Years

Instructions for writing this section. *Start by answering the questions about your life in your adult years. This period would be from the time that you were about twenty until you were about forty. For many people, their adult years include the period of time when they received advanced education, pre-career training, entered the workforce, and started families. Remember to include the years that this period of your life covered.*

After you have recorded the details and memories from your personal life, choose three memory prompts from the Moments in History section and copy each prompt onto one of the Memorable Moment lines in this section. Then, answer the prompt in the section below this Memorable Moment. The Moments in History that we have selected are only suggestions. You may add another important or historical event from this period of your life.

The goal of this section is to understand this period of history through your eyes. Some prompts list multiple people or things. You can choose one from these lists or add one of your own.

🖋 My adult years were during the years _____ to _____

🖋 In my adult years, I had a pet _____ named _____.

  A special memory about my pet is _____

  _____

🖋 A special family memory from my adult years is _____

  _____

  _____

  _____

  _____

List the places and dates of birth or adoption for each of your children in the spaces below

🖊 My child/childrenwas/were born

_____ on _____ in _____
    (name)   the parent of your grandchild

_____ on _____ in _____
    (name)

_____ on _____ in _____
    (name)

_____ on _____ in _____
    (name)

_____ on _____ in _____
    (name)

_____ on _____ in _____
    (name)

🖊 We chose your parent's name because _____

🖊 A special memory from the time that your parent was a baby is

_____

_____

_____

_____

🖊 A memorable incident when your parent was a young child was

_____

_____

_____

_____

🖊 In my adult years, I made a living as _____

🖋 A special memory from my career during this period is

_____

_____

_____

_____

🖋 An important thing that I did to prepare myself for my career was

_____

_____

_____

_____

🖋 The part of my work that I enjoyed the most was

_____

_____

_____

_____

🖋 The parts of my work that I didn't like were

_____

_____

_____

_____

🖋 During my adult years, I'm proud that I

_____

_____

_____

_____

In my adult years, my favorite interests, hobbies, or sports were

_____

_____

_____

_____

A special place that I visited during my adult years was _____

The visit was special because

_____

_____

_____

_____

If I could relive my adult years, something I would do differently would be

_____

_____

_____

_____

One thing that I didn't do enough in my adult years was

_____

_____

_____

_____

🖋 One thing that I'm really glad that I did in my adult years was

_____

_____

_____

_____

🖋 An important relationship that I developed in my adult years was with

_____ because _____

_____

_____

_____

_____

🖋 A favorite song from my adult years was _____

🖋 A favorite movie from my adult years was _____

🖋 One of the most memorable books that I read was _____

because _____

_____

_____

_____

🖋 One of the most important lessons that I learned during my adult years was

_____

_____

_____

_____

The World in My Adult Years

Life was much cheaper in my adult years…

🖋 A house in my neighborhood cost _____

🖋 A car cost _____

🖋 Lunch at a restaurant that I might have visited cost _____

🖋 A movie ticket cost _____

Important historical events that influenced my adult years included:

🖋 _____

🖋 _____

🖋 _____

🖋 _____

🖋 _____

Memorable Moment #1 from My Adult Years

Copy one of the memory prompts on this line. Answer it below.

_____

_____

_____

_____

_____

_____

_____

_____

Memorable Moment #2 from My Adult Years

Copy one of the memory prompts on this line. Answer it below.

_____

_____

_____

_____

_____

_____

_____

_____

Memorable Moment #3 from My Adult Years

Copy one of the memory prompts on this line. Answer it below.

Moments in History: 1980s

During the 1980s, phones and computers shrank, and Apple MacIntosh sprouted. Earthquakes rocked California and Mexico City and added to a stream of natural and man-made disasters, including Chernobyl, Mount St. Helens, and the Exxon Valdez oil spill. *Star Wars* movies continued to thrive on the big screen, and MTV, the Home Shopping Network, and Oprah came to TV. Activism took on Apartheid in South Africa and LGBTQ rights in the US. "Preppy yuppies" were style setters. And finally, the Berlin Wall came down. Let me share my memories of the events, people, products, sports, and art that shaped this decade.

prince michael jordan | michael jackson | george michael | diego maradona | michael jordan | lady diana
michael jordan | margaret thatcher | diego maradona | manuel noriega
magic johnson | the police | exxon valdez | chernobyl | george michael
big bang | berlin wall | madonna | john elway | prince | prince | big bang | lady diana
margaret thatcher | michael jordan | berlin wall | wham | chernobyl | prince
the police | patrick ewing | the police | wham | prince | big bang | george vadez
john elway | patrick ewing | lady diana | lady diana
chernobyl | george michael | the police | the police
mount st. helens | michael jackson | berlin wall
prince | chernobyl | lady diana | john elway | magic johnson | margaret thatcher
manuel noriega | michael jackson | patrick ewing | exxon valdez | michael jackson | ronald reagan
diego maradona | george michael | magic johnson | wham
mount st. helens | madonna | wham | magic johnson | big bang
michael jackson | mount st. helens | berlin wall | michael jordan
ronald reagan | manuel noriega | exxon valdez | the police | ronald reagan
the police | margaret thatcher | ronald reagan
wham
margaret thatcher

1980s Memory Prompts

Choose three memory prompts below or use one of the important historical events that influenced a period of your life. Copy and answer the prompt as one of the three Memorable Moments that follow your personal memories for this period. If have memories that were shared with you by family members, you can include those as well. The goal of this section is to understand this period of history through your eyes. Some prompts list multiple people or things. You can choose one from these lists or add one of your own.

- A memory about Ronald Reagan's presidency is…

- A memory about Margaret Thatcher is…

- A memory about the fall of the Berlin Wall is…

- A memory about the Iran-Contra scandal is…

- A memory of the British miners' strike is…

- A memory of the Chernobyl disaster is…

- A memory of the Falklands War is…

- A memory about a sports event or sports figure from the 1980s such as Chris Evert, Roger Clemens, Wayne Gretzky, Magic Johnson, Joe Montana, Mike Tyson, Larry Bird, Sugar Ray Leonard, Patrick Ewing, John Elway, Michael Jordan, Mary Lou Retton, Carl Lewis, Diego Maradona and the 1986 World Cup, is…

- A memory about a natural disaster that occurred in the 1980s such as the Loma Prieta earthquake, Hurricane Hugo, Mount St. Helens, the Mexico City earthquake, the Exxon Valdez oil spill, is…

- A memory about a science or technology breakthrough in the 1980s such as the artificial heart, the discovery of the *Titanic*, DNA fingerprinting, is…

- A memory about a new product that appeared in the 1980s such as disposable cameras, Gameboy, Apple Macintosh, unleaded gasoline, MTV, CD players, camcorders, Microsoft Windows, Motorola DynaTAC series mobile phones, fax machines, *USA Today*, Swatch watches, boomboxes, Cabbage Patch dolls, Home Shopping Network, is…

🖊 A memory about a popular movie star in the 1980s such as Emilio Estevez, Dan Ackroyd, Carrie Fisher, James Earl Jones, Eddie Murphy, Bill Murray, Steve Martin, Sigourney Weaver, Glenn Close, Tom Cruise, Jamie Lee Curtis, is…

🖊 A memory about a popular musician or band in the 1980s such as Michael Jackson, Prince, Madonna, U2, Bruce Springsteen, Run DMC, The Police, Public Enemy, Whitney Houston, Lionel Richie, Phil Collins, Van Halen, N.W.A., LL Cool J, is…

🖊 A memory of a big social movement in the 1980s such as Yuppies, Reaganomics, anti-Apartheid, ACTUP LGBTQ activism, homelessness, preppy style, the New Age movement, the anti-nuclear movement, is…

Moments in History: 1990s

In the 1990s, wars tore through the Gulf and Bosnia. UK leaders pushed for peace with the Belfast Accords. Apartheid ended, and Nelson Mandela walked free. O.J. Simpson got in trouble—and so did US President Bill Clinton. Scientists and activists sounded the global warming alarm; few people listened. The Internet began connecting us and changed our daily lives forever. Let me tell you how events, people, products, sports, and art in the 1990s changed my life and view of the world.

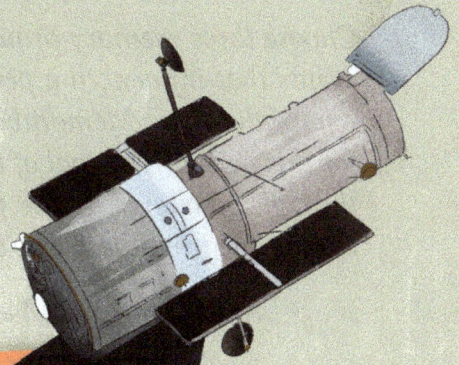

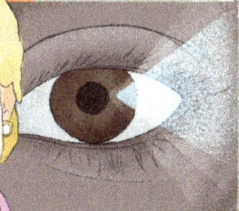

1990s Memory Prompts

Choose three memory prompts below or use one of the important historical events that influenced a period of your life. Copy and answer the prompt as one of the three Memorable Moments that follow your personal memories for this period. The goal of this section is to understand this period of history through your eyes. Some prompts list multiple people or things. You can choose one from these lists or add one of your own.

- A memory about Nelson Mandela or Apartheid in South Africa is…

- A memory about the launch of the Internet is…

- A memory about President Bill Clinton is…

- A memory about the Gulf War is…

- A memory about the Bosnian War is…

- A memory about the collapse of the Soviet Union is…

- A memory about the O.J. Simpson trial is…

- A memory about the Oklahoma City bombing is…

- A memory about the Belfast Accords is…

- A memory of Princess Diana is…

- A memory about a sports event or sports figure from the 1990s such as Andre Agassi, Mark McGuire, Sammy Sosa, Brett Favre, Mia Hamm, Michelle Kwan, Dennis Rodman, Monica Seles, Bo Jackson, Ronaldo Luis, Nazario de Lima, Ken Griffey Jr. Tiger Woods, Charles Barkley, Derek Jeter, Dale Earnhardt, Zinedine Zidane, Mark Messier, Eric Cantona, Cal Ripken, is…

- A memory about a natural disaster that occurred in the 1990s such as Hurricane Andrew, the Northridge earthquake, the Mt. Pinatubo eruption, the Kobe earthquake, the Izmit earthquake, the Bangladesh cyclone, is…

- A memory about a science or technology breakthrough in the 1990s such as the launch of the Hubble Space Telescope, launch of the Human Genome Project, the Linux operating system, the global warming alarm, Lasik surgery, the Channel Tunnel, is…

- A memory about a new product that appeared in the 1990s such as Netscape Navigator (the first Internet browser), text messaging, Adobe Photoshop, Sony PlayStation, Nintendo 64, Tamagotchi, DVDs, Google, MP3s, Reebok Pumps, G-Shock watches, Palm Pilots, Blackberrys, Motorola beepers, Doc Martens, Sony Discman, Beanie Babies, starter jackets, ebooks, digital cameras, is…

- A memory about a popular movie or TV star in the 1990s such as Tom Hanks, Leonardo DiCaprio, Bruce Willis, Samuel L. Jackson, Robin Williams, Whoopi Goldberg, Julia Roberts, Mel Gibson, Arnold Schwarzenegger, Al Pacino, Michelle Pfeiffer, Brad Pitt, Richard Gere, Keanu Reeves, Sharon Stone, Sandra Bullock, Demi Moore, Jodie Foster, is…

- A memory about a popular musician or band in the 1990s such as Nirvana, Pearl Jam, Tupac, Dr. Dre, Radiohead, Mariah Carey, Notorious B.I.G., Britney Spears, Garth Brooks, Spice Girls, Shania Twain, Celine Dion, Eminem, is…

- A memory of a big social movement in the 1990s such as mass shootings, gay rights, the Million Man March, the Los Angeles Riots, is…

My Middle Age Years

Instructions for writing this section. *Start by answering the questions about your life in your middle age years. This period would be from the time that you were about forty until you were about sixty. Remember to include the years that this period of your life covered.*

After you have recorded the details and memories from your personal life, choose three memory prompts from the Moments in History section and copy each prompt onto one of the Memorable Moment lines in this section. Then, answer the prompt in the section below this Memorable Moment. The Moments in History that we have selected are only suggestions. You may add another important or historical event from this period of your life.

The goal of this section is to understand this period of history through your eyes. Some prompts list multiple people or things. You can choose one from these lists or add one of your own.

🖋 My middle age years were during the years _____ to _____

🖋 In my middle age years, my favorite interests, hobbies, or sports were

_____

_____

_____

🖋 In my middle age years, I had a pet _____ named _____.

A special memory about my pet is _____

_____

_____

_____

_____

🖋 A special memory from career during this period is _____

_____

_____

_____

_____

🖋 A special family memory from my middle age years is _____

_____

_____

_____

_____

🖋 A special place that I visited during my middle age years is _____

🖋 My visit was memorable because _____

_____

_____

_____

_____

🖋 A favorite movie from my middle age years was _____

🖋 During my middle age years, I learned that _____

_____

_____

_____

_____

The World in My Middle Age Years

Life was cheaper in my middle age years…

🪶 A house in my neighborhood cost _____

🪶 A car cost _____

🪶 Lunch at a restaurant that I might have visited cost _____

🪶 A movie ticket cost _____

Important historical events that influenced my middle age years included:

🪶 _____

🪶 _____

🪶 _____

🪶 _____

🪶 _____

Memorable Moment #1 from My Middle Age Years

Copy one of the memory prompts on this line. Answer it below.

_____

_____

_____

_____

_____

_____

_____

Memorable Moment #2 from My Middle Age Years

Copy one of the memory prompts on this line. Answer it below.

_____

_____

_____

_____

_____

_____

_____

Memorable Moment #3 from My Middle Age Years

Copy one of the memory prompts on this line. Answer it below.

Moments in History: 2000s

People feared the year 2000 – would computers stop and bring the world to a halt? But the decade opened quietly. The 9/11 terrorists ripped apart that calm. A turbulent ten years would come next as natural disasters like Hurricane Katrina, the 2004 Christmas Tsunami, the Sichuan earthquake in China, and the European heat wave upended millions of lives. Portable technology in iPods, iPhones, USB flash drives, and Bitcoin let us do more and more on the move. Myspace, Twitter, Facebook, and LinkedIn connected us and redefined "friends" and "likes". Let me share my memories of the events, people, products, sports, and art that the 2000s brought to life.

2000s Memory Prompts

Choose three memory prompts below or use one of the important historical events that influenced a period of your life. Copy and answer the prompt as one of the three Memorable Moments that follow your personal memories for this period. The goal of this section is to understand this period of history through your eyes. Some prompts list multiple people or things. You can choose one from these lists or add one of your own.

- ✎ A memory about the 9/11 attacks is…

- ✎ A memory about the 2004 Christmas tsunami is…

- ✎ A memory about the 2005 London bombings is…

- ✎ A memory about Hurricane Katrina is…

- ✎ A memory of the Global Financial Crisis is…

- ✎ A memory about President Barack Obama is…

- ✎ A memory of Fidel Castro stepping down as Cuba's leader is…

- ✎ A memory about a sports event or sports figure from the 2000s such as Serena Williams, Albert Pujols, Shaquille O'Neal, Peyton Manning, Roger Federer, Michael Phelps, Martin Brodeur, Thierry Henry, Derek Jeter, Alex Rodriguez, Kobe Bryant, Usain Bolt, Ronaldinho, Tom Brady, is…

- ✎ A memory about a natural disaster that occurred in the 2000s such as Hurricane Charley, the Sichuan earthquake, the Pakistan earthquake, the Europe heat wave, is…

- ✎ A memory about a science or technology breakthrough in the 2000s such as Segways, virtual keyboards, hybrid cars, dark matter, retinal implants, Nintendo Wii, is…

- ✎ A memory about a new product that appeared in the 2000s such as Wikipedia, iPhone, Bitcoin, iPod, Twitter, Facebook, YouTube, Netflix, GPS, USB flash drive, noise-cancelling headsets, is…

A memory about a popular movie or TV star in the 2000s such as Russell Crowe, Orlando Bloom, Will Smith, George Clooney, Denzel Washington, Cate Blanchett, Elizabeth Banks, Emma Watson, Johnny Depp, Angelina Jolie, Cameron Diaz, is…

A memory about a popular musician or band in the 2000s such as Britney Spears, Christina Aguilera, U2, Pearl Jam, Red Hot Chili Peppers, Eminem, Justin Timberlake, Linkin Park, Outkast, Kanye West, Jay Z, Usher, Beyonce, Radiohead, Coldplay, is…

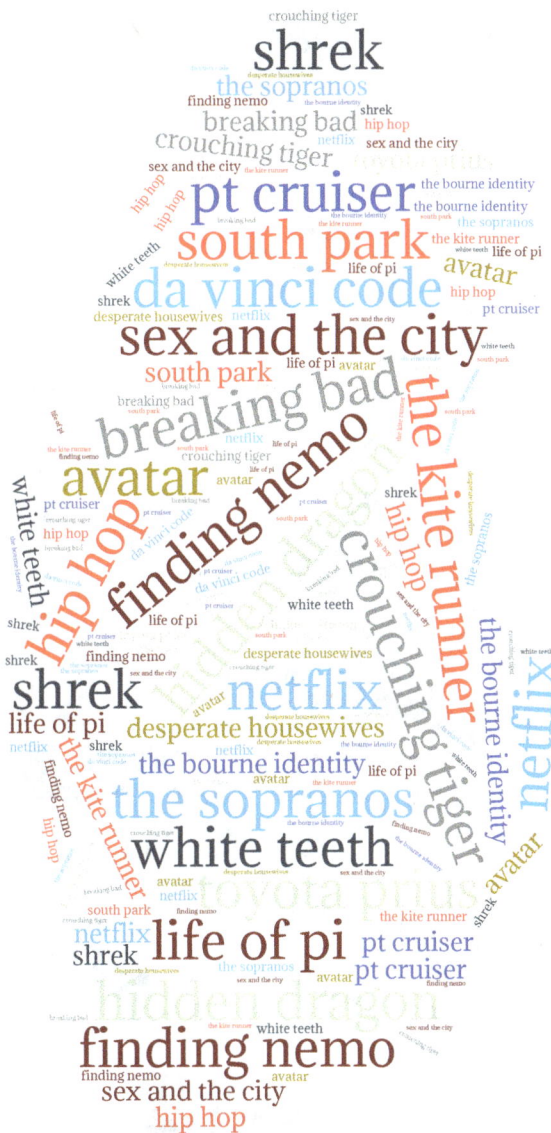

My Later Years

Instructions for writing this section. *Start by answering the questions about your life in your later years. This period would be from the time after you were sixty years old. Remember to include the years that this period of your life covered.*

After you have recorded the details and memories from your personal life, choose three memory prompts from the Moments in History section and copy each prompt onto one of the Memorable Moment lines in this section. Then, answer the prompt in the section below this Memorable Moment. The Moments in History that we have selected are only suggestions. You may add another important or historical event from this period of your life.

The goal of this section is to understand this period of history through your eyes. Some prompts list multiple people or things. You can choose one from these lists or add one of your own.

🪶 My later years were during the years _____ to _____

🪶 In my later years, my favorite interests, hobbies, or sports were

_____

_____

_____

🪶 In my later years, I had a pet _____ named_____.

A special memory about my pet is _____

_____

_____

_____

A special family memory from my later years is _____

_____

_____

_____

_____

A special place that I visited during my later years is _____

My visit was memorable because _____

_____

_____

_____

_____

During my later years, I learned that _____

_____

_____

_____

_____

One thing I'm glad I did when I was young is _____

because _____

_____

_____

_____

_____

🖋 One thing that I wish I had done when I was young is _____

because _____

_____

_____

_____

_____

🖋 An important life achievement for me is _____

because _____

_____

_____

_____

🖋 A favorite movie from my later years is _____

🖋 A favorite book from my later years is _____

The World in My Later Years

Life was cheaper in my later years…

- A house in my neighborhood cost _____
- A car cost _____
- Lunch at a restaurant that I might have visited cost _____
- A movie ticket cost _____

Important historical events that influenced my later years included:

- _____
- _____
- _____
- _____
- _____

Memorable Moment #1 from My Later Years

Copy one of the memory prompts on this line. Answer it below.

_____

_____

_____

_____

_____

_____

_____

Memorable Moment #2 from My Later Years

Copy one of the memory prompts on this line. Answer it below.

_____

_____

_____

_____

_____

_____

_____

Memorable Moment #3 from My Later Years

Copy one of the memory prompts on this line. Answer it below.

_____

_____

_____

_____

_____

_____

_____

_____

A Timelin[e]

1950s

1940s

1960s

# of Memories

SPIRIT OF 76

1970s

1980s

PUNK

1990s

2000s

_____ _____ _____

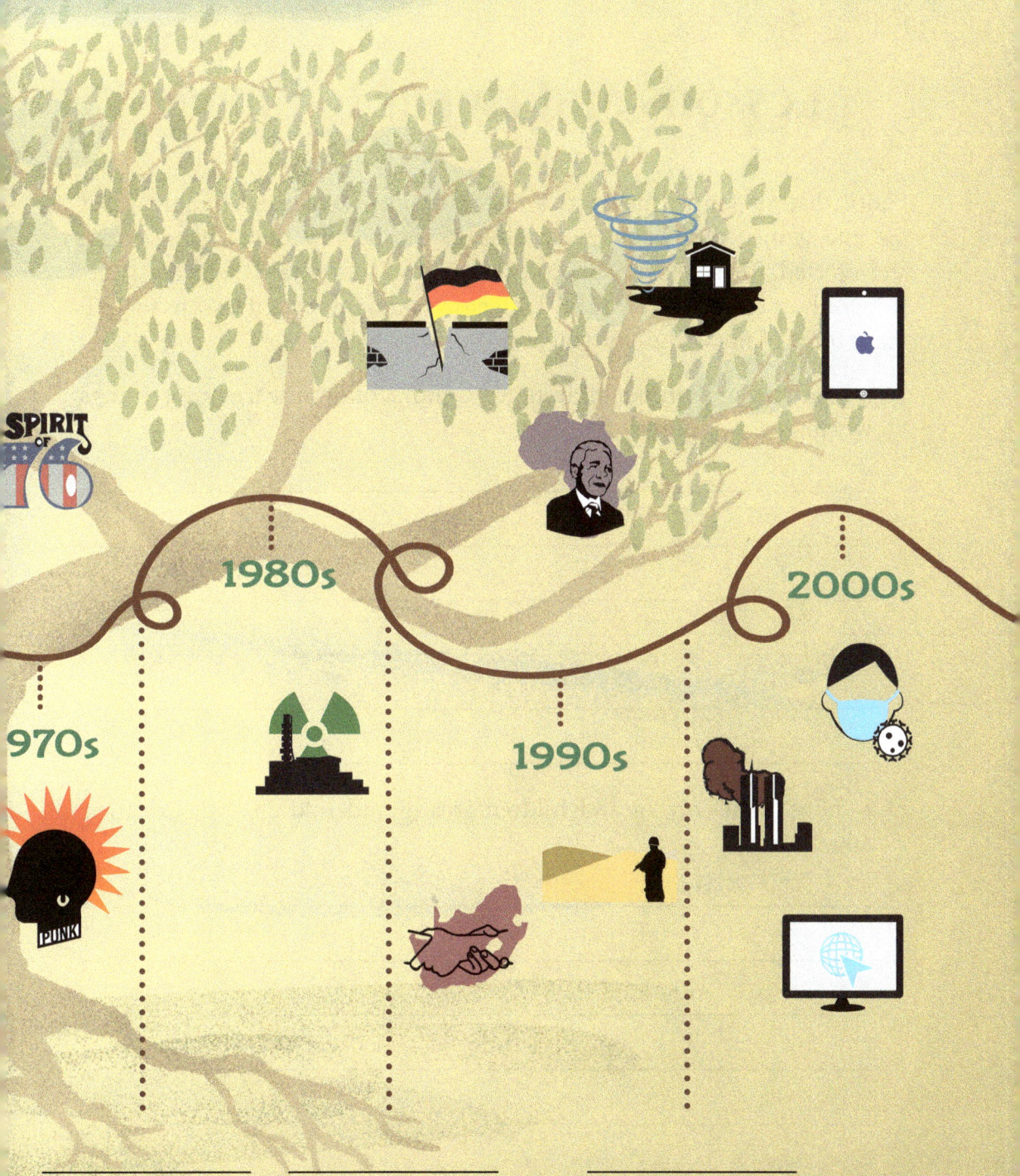

Add your own milestone events on these blank lines.

Lessons and Hopes to Share

I hope that my family members and community have learned more about me and gained a new understanding of the history that I experienced and created. These events, people, places, and journeys have shaped me. Hopefully, they will leave you with memories and important lessons too. I'll share some of my wishes for you and your lives below.

✐ I hope that my grandchildren/great-grandchildren learn these things when they're children

_____

_____

_____

_____

_____

_____

✐ I hope that my grandchildren/great-grandchildren pursue their education by

_____

_____

_____

_____

_____

_____

I hope that you'll visit some of these places

_____

_____

_____

_____

_____

I hope that you develop a career that enables you to

_____

_____

_____

_____

_____

I hope that you find a partner who

_____

_____

_____

_____

_____

🖋 I hope that you contribute to your community and the world around you by

_____

_____

_____

_____

_____

_____

🖋 I hope that you'll remember this favorite quote or saying of mine

_____

_____

_____

_____

_____

_____

www.ingramcontent.com/pod-product-compliance
Lightning Source LLC
Chambersburg PA
CBHW080757300326
41914CB00055B/927